Eye Shadow Techniques

Amazing and good looking eye shadow techniques for every kind of eye shapes.

By: Jennifer

Table of Content

===================================

Introduction to Eye shadow

Eye shadow is the important part of our makeup. There are different colors in eye shades. Eye shade comes in different types. Eye shadow comes in powder and cream forms. Powder eye shadow can be applied with brush and cream eye shadow can be applied with brush or finger. Eye shadow can applied in different colors and textures. You can soften your regard, Create a mood and improve your eye shape, depends on the look you want. To get best result, you can choose the right color.

What is eye shadow ????????

Eye shadow is a that type of colored make-up which is put on the eyelids to make the eyes more beautiful. Eye shadow is a cosmetic powder or cream in different colors which is apply to the eyelids of eyes.

How To Apply Eye shadow

Step 1and 2

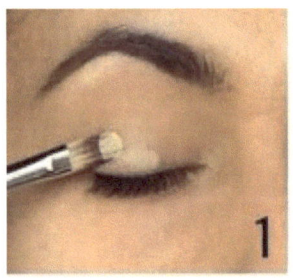 

Start by cleaning the area around the eyes. First apply a moisturizer or an eye cream and massage it. Then prepare the eye area with an eye primer so that the makeup stays put for a long time and gives a smoothly finish. You can also apply concealer that matches the skin tone around your eyes. Apply the concealer with a brush and cover it with a transparent powder. This will, make the skin crease-proof, and also conceal any discoloration of the skin.

You should always observe the shape of your eyes and decide on a makeup technique that will make them beautiful. The eye area consists of the eyelid, the crease, and the brow bone. It is also important that you know which shade is to use on each of these areas. Use shades like frost, shimmer, shine on the eyelid and brow bone, and matte finish textures on the crease.

Start by applying the color on the eyelid with a flat eye shadow applicator brush using a sweeping motion. I have used a dull gold shade in frost texture, because I have very less lid space. This lighter shade will make my eyelid more prominent. Start the application from the center and then sweep it towards both inner and outer corners. Apply the color clearly on the lid and deposit more for intensity.

Step 3and 4

Thirdly we can concentrate on the crease area of eye. Use a darker shade of eye shadow to define the eye shape. To get this, go for shades like deep browns, black, deep gray, dark purple, etc. Start applying from the outer corner of the eye, making a 'V', and blend it half the eyelid with a fluffy eye shadow blending brush. Keep blending until the color starts to look softer. In order to highlight the brow bone, go for lighter shades like frost or shiny textures.

Fourthly To make the eye makeup more dramatic, use a kohl pencil on the lower lash line. blend it with a pencil brush if you want a smoky effect.
use a white colored eye pencil on the lower rims of the eyes is the best way to make them look bigger and fresher. Apply eyeliner to define the eyes. Start from the outer corner and pull it inwards using small strokes.

Step 5and 6

Next , Apply eyeliner to define the eyes. Start from the outer corner and slowly pull it inwards using small strokes. Wear the eyeliner as you like – you can keep it simple, or make it dramatic.

Then, Apply two to three coats of mascara to complete the eye makeup. To take it up a point, you can also wear artificial lashes and coat them with mascara.
And that's the final look of your eyes.

Some tips To Apply Eye shadow:

❖ To avoid eyeshade fall out, powder the area under your eyes with a transparent powder before starting the eye makeup. Once you are done, just sweep the powder off.
❖ It is always good to finish your eye makeup first and then move on to your base makeup, you can quickly clean it up without spoiling your base makeup.
❖ To define the crease area, use a pencil brush and then blend it with a fluffy brush.
❖ Choose an eyeshade formula that works best for you. They are available in cream, powder, or pressed form. Cream eyeshades can be used as a base for powder eye shadows.
❖ If you have difficult to drawing the 'V' on the outer corner of the eyes, then draw a '#' with an eye pencil and blend it immediately to avoid stark corners.
❖ Apply a good base or primer as it will make the eyeshade stay put for a long time

.

Best Eye Shadow Colors for Blue Eyes

Eye Shadow for Blue Eyes

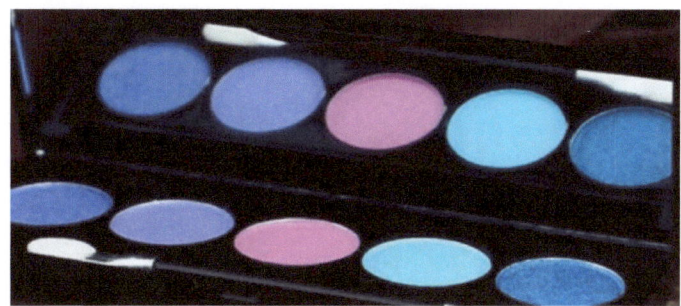

Girls with blue eyes can enhance their eyes. different colors, however, can really bring out blue eyes better than others. When selecting eye shadow shades, test your skin tone and hair color as well as the actual blue shade of your eyes. What may look great on a blue-eyed beauty .

Orange Eye Shadow for Blue Eyes

orange shadow is unflattering eye shadow . Orange-based shades are some of the best choices in eye shadow for blue eyes. Orange-based shapes provide a contrast to blue eyes that really makes the color pop. You don't have to wear a bright or neon orange, though.
Consider the eye shadow shades such as:

- ❖ Rust
- ❖ Copper
- ❖ Peach
- ❖ Coral
- ❖ Bronze

Cool Eye Shadows for Blue Eyes

Many women with blue eyes look fabulous with cool eye shadow shades.

Some great choices are:

- ❖ Pale to medium blue
- ❖ Purple
- ❖ Deep or midnight blue
- ❖ Pale pink shades
- ❖ Violet

Blue Eyes with Pale Blue Shadow

women that using a dark shade of blue will actually bring the more natural blue tones in the eye for creating a brighter and more vibrant look. Turquoise shades can also work for blue eyes. girls with blue eyes that have a touch of green or hazel, teal shades can bring out green tint for a fresh and good look. be careful not to do these bright hues. Violets are most recommended for women with a combination of baby blues and blonde hair. because a light purple is smoothie for most blondes with fair skin. Brunettes love them also, so do not rule them out right away if you have dark hair.

You can also use violet on the creases of your eyelids. A lighter lavender above the crease will give you a more dramatic look . More neutral colors are ideal for daytime, but it is always fun to wear purple no matter what the time or season.

Neutral Shadows for Blue Eyes

Blue Eyes with Brown Shadow

Most of the neutral shades, such as taupe and champagne, looks good with blue eyes and work very well for a natural look. Tans can flatter the shape and shade of your eyes without overpowering your hair or other features, and most brown shadow shades are very pleasing colors for blue eyes. Such as:

- ❖ Khaki colored shadow
- ❖ Chocolate brown
- ❖ Grey shades
- ❖ Camel shadow

It can blessed with naturally red hair, brown shades will tend to work beautifully on your blue eyes. then your hair is already such a vibrant color, your skin tone and eyes will demand a more natural looking shadow. if you really love color. Just start with small accents and work your way up to the level that works best for you.

Evening Eye Shadow

Black eye shades can be too much for daytime, but it can provide you an intense contrast to blue eyes that really makes them stand out for evening. Use black shadow for smoky eye look or placed along the upper lid for emphasis. If you are looking for more dramatic evening look, mixing black liner with a bright blue will give you a classic "smoky" effect. You can also throw in some silver, or turquoise if you are going out and want a funky nighttime feel.

gold shimmer shadow is also a pretty evening option for those with gorgeous blue eyes.

The Best Shadows for Blue-Grey Eyes

There are almost no right or wrong color for blue-grey eyes.

- ❖ Metallic gold
- ❖ Peach
- ❖ Coral
- ❖ Metallic copper

these shades will contrast with not only the blue, but also the coolness of the grey in your eyes. If you want more wide-eyed look or even a subtle, smoky look, then try:

- ❖ Charcoal
- ❖ Black
- ❖ Sheer violet
- ❖ pink

Pair the shadows with black, charcoal grey, or liner on top and line the waterline with white for an innocent, wide-eyed look. for a smoky, nighttime overshadow look, use black liner along the top and bottom, blend out with black shadow, then line the waterline with black.

The Best Shadows for Blue-Green Eyes

Purple-toned shadows will bring out the most fabulous look in your eye color, so try it:

- ❖ Blue-toned pinks
- ❖ Warm pinks or corals
- ❖ Royal purple
- ❖ Plum
- ❖ Eggplant
- ❖ Burgundy
- ❖ Reddish-browns
- ❖ Violet

shades with purplish or reddish undertones will provide greater contrast and make the green more clear in your eye color. If that feels too vibrant, dark, or just otherwise out of your comfort zone, try:

- ❖ Shimmering
- ❖ Khaki
- ❖ sheer greenish-gold

These shades will pick up on the green in your eyes. It can look as if your eyes are sparkling a bit more than usual but it cannot be the same dramatic contrast that the purple shades.
You cannot go wrong with bronze, when your eyes are blue. Just make sure you don't go too warm if your skin tone is cool or neutral.

How to Buy Shadow for Blue Eyes

Many women prefer the latter because it takes the guesswork out of finding coordinating base, crease, and highlight shades when we go to shop there are many brands to choose from. You can choose individual shadows and experiment with different color combinations, or you can purchase pre-designed shadow palettes for blue eyes.
You can purchase eye shadow designed for blue eyes which makes it easy to select gorgeous quality makeup made to make your eyes look their best.

- ❖ warm brown, rust brown, golden bronze, and deep brown, all warm tones that are perfect for adding a spark to blue eyes.
- ❖ You probably only need one or the other, not both, so consider the undertones in the shadows.
- ❖ The shadows include Amber Lights, which is specifically designed for those with fair skin and light eyes. Consider creating your own palette with that one, Coppering, Corduroy Type.

Blue eyes are gorgeous in everything from warm-toned neutrals with a hint of peach to contrast with the blue, to the smokiest of all gray shadow. Test a few colors against your skin tone to see which ones not only bring out your eyes but help create a flattering look on your skin tone as well.

How To Do Makeup For Grey Eyes

Taking the case of grey eyes, the blue eyes, the browns and the greens or black eyes for that matter, the shades would range from the palest to the darkest. This is exactly why makeup should be customized as per the shades and hues you have been blessed with, which enhances the look and creates individualism at large.

Stand in front of the mirror and wear a white shirt under bright light to do this though, as the white glare would create a spectrum that shows you the real shade of grey you have been blessed with. But first there are a few colors with makeup that grey-eyed lasses should completely avoid.

- ❖ Peach
- ❖ Metal and light grey eyeshades
- ❖ pink
- ❖ Bold and bright shades

Women With Bluish-Grey Eyes:

The color wheel will give you an idea on which color would compliment and not contrast the bluish-grey touch in your iris. Like opposite on the color wheel, orange compliments the shade of blue in your iris. So the shades which you can choose other than orange would be peaches in matte, metal copper tones, etc.

Women With Greenish-Grey Eyes:

In color wheel shows red would contrast the green and would not make the eyes look subtle, soft, hence avoiding the shade and all hues under its umbrella would be the best thing to do. shades that you could doll up your eyes with are colors from almonds to salmon, purples to orchids, and even plums to deep caramels.

Women With Brown And Hazel Grey Eyes:

Some women's have brown and hazel touches along with the dominant grey eyes on our iris, which is the use of purple eyeshade would work best as a complementing shade. Other colors that would work like magic are tan, mocha, chocolate and brownish metal tones.

A Touch Of Dark Grey

Grey eye shadow is for a sophisticated look.

- ❖ If you apply a very dark shade of eyeliner and with grey eye shadow, the look on the eyes would be very light.
- ❖ There are many other shades of grey shadow for the lids to be applied. For example, a medium shade in grey or a mix of two different grey shades, which would be closest to your eye color, can be used.
- ❖ If you apply a very light shade of eyeliner with the grey eye shadow, the eyes will look smoky-dark.

Use Silver And Black

Silver and black mix for the eyes is an excellent choice, but you really should keep the shimmer on the lids to the minimum. It all depends on the occasion, and the event. Black smoky eyes are haute especially if the iris is a pale canvas. Mix a little pink or peach to silver eyeliner, for the pale iris to have something to complement it with, and work your way to the party look this season.

Makeup For Brown Eyes

Now start brown eye make up, With the help of a yellow or white highlighter, the brow area needs to be touched first with a stroke of highlighter. The shade should be touched just once and very gently to form the base. Blend the shade into the brow bone on both eyes.

Step1:

Take the lightest brown shade and color of the upper eyes, one at a time. You should first focus with gentle strokes on the outer eye corner and then go towards the inside of the eyes. Culminate around the inner eye corner and repeat on the other eye.

Step2:

Go to the upper lash line and use a brown stencil to give a half stroke and a very light touch to the area .

Step3:

Go to the lower lash line, and for both your eyes, use two strokes of the brown stencil and line them well and thick.

Step 4:

Use a red liner and get the water lines of the eyes, up and down, with a stroke each to color them one at a time

Step 5:

Use an eye shadow brush that would help you blend the colors of the lash line and the water line, the red and brown stencil strokes for the upper and lower eyelids. Now, from the outer corner, blend inwards and to the crease, then to the socket. you can start from the middle and then to the left, and from the left to the middle and then to the right!

Step 6:

The final touch of brown for a caramel look is just one last stroke for the upper and lower lash lines would be enough.

Hazel Eyes

Hazel eyes are very beautiful eyes. hazel eyes reflect the colors around them, and they seem to change in color from gold, light brown, green, blue, and even gray, according to hair, makeup, and clothing colors. The beauty of hazel is not only the lovely, unique color, but also that there are so many different ways to play up this eye color.
Hazel eyes may have a brown ring around the pupil .Hazel eyes are a combination of green, gold, and brown. these shadow palettes are flattering:

* ❖ Peach, beige, and taupe
* ❖ Gold, bronze, and copper
* ❖ Deep and mossy greens

When hazel eyes look brown, these shadows work well:

* ❖ Gray, silver, and charcoal
* ❖ Bronze and gold
* ❖ Violet, lavender, and blue

try these eye shadow combinations which have a blue tint:

- ❖ Gray, silver, and copper
- ❖ Pink, rose, and lavender
- ❖ Charcoal, black, and brown

Makeup to Make Hazel Eyes

There are as many types to use makeup to make hazel eyes stand out, including considering the individual colors.

Gold Flecks:

Use a light shade from lash line to brow, then a medium gold shade in the crease, smudge a darker shade along the lashes. Finish with black eye liner and mascara, and watch those honey-colored swirls stand out.

Green Flecks:

A shimmery bronze color palette will also accent the green in hazel eyes. Apply the lightest as a base from lashes to brows, the medium one in the crease, and the darkest along the lash line. For daytime, choose a neutral shade that matches your skin tone, and apply the three lightest colors of that shade in the same manner as for the evening look.

Blue Flecks:

Blue flecks in hazel eyes are quite uncommon, and if you will want to play them up with a purple or plum eye shadow palette

Brown Tones

You will want to stick with brown eye shadows in various intensities, brown eye liner, and rich brown mascara.

Green Smokey Eye Makeup:

Material Used:

- ❖ Eye shadow Base
- ❖ eyeliner pencil in the shade Green Grenade to be used as the base.
- ❖ Eyeliner in the shade Glazed Green to be used on the upper lash line
- ❖ Eye Shadow
- ❖ Black Kajal
- ❖ Faces Eye Shadow
- ❖ eye shadow in the shade Saddle Brown.

Method :

First Start off with a good base .Clean your eyes with a cotton pad to remove any dirt of old makeup. Then prime your eyes with Eye shadow base over your eye lids. Apply the Green Grenade pencil as a base over your eye lids. Apply the Khaki Green color on your crease Apply the dark green shade on your lid. Then Blend both the shades properly. Make sure that the color is blended in seamlessly. Apply the eyeliner in the shade Glazed Green on your upper lash line. Blend this slightly.

Now take any brown or black eye shadow of your choice. Blend this in on the outer "V" portion and also on your outer lid. Finish off your look with any highlighter, kajal. If you are not comfortable with mascara then you can simply darken your lashes by doing a tight lining of the lashes.

This is a very simple to create look, it does give the eyes a wonderful professionally look. Another thing to always remember is to blend in all colors nicely, as you don't want any lines or crease on your makeup.

Smokey Eye Makeup For Small And Big Eyes

There are a few tips for choosing smoky makeup effect for different shapes of eyes:

To make smaller eyes look bigger

Smokey eye makeup tips for smaller eyes:

Some people have small eyes as compared of their face. Smoky eyes for small eyes has a whole different approach to it. if you have small eyes then these tips are helpful for you:

In first step you have to use a concealer on the eye lids, not necessarily on to creases but a must on the brow bones. If you might be having dark circles, it is very important to cover them up. may apply small little dots of foundation and blend well on the part Make sure that you use not too dark a brown or black or bronze or purple for smoky eyes when your eye's are small.

Next, Do not use the dark color all over your eye lids. Use an applicator to use the dark color only from half end of the eyes extending towards the brows but not reaching them in a tail. Then use a lighter color to make eyes pop out on to the frontal lids. Line your upper lids with a very thin line of liner. a shade near to black but not jet black. Now take a shimmer white or silver eye pencil and just put a dot between the nose and the eyes. Also just below the brow cover the area with silver shimmer to high light the brow bone. If your lashes are small. Do a double curling before and after mascara application for both the upper and lower lashes.

Smokey Eye makeup tips for Big and elongated eyes:

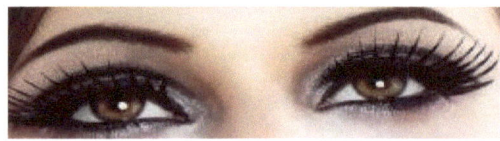

Smokey eyes on big eyes are simple and easy to do. You can even play with darkest of shades and also multiple shades at the same time by blending 3-4 colors together. Use concealer and foundation.

Next use darker shade like black for bronze or dark purple for mauve and so on to the crease. Now blend up this darker shade to a shade near t black from the extreme end point of crease extending in a tail to just below the brow bones. Then Use a very small amount of shimmer white on to brow bones and that too in a thin line just below the brows. Use a liner in a darker shade Line the under rim line. Just make them proportionate by using kajal or liner whatever you want.

After that use mascara along with false lashes if you want to go for big dark eyes .If your lashes are good enough, double curling is not required. Use mascara on both the upper and lower lashes .You can also use just a small tiny dot of shimmer white pencil for that start point of eyes near the nose. Remember the more darker shades you use, the smaller your eyes look.

Scalloped Eye Makeup

 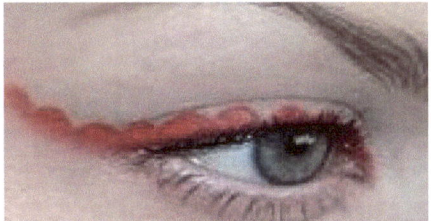

Material Used:

There is the list of products, which are use to make the scalloped eye makeup look:

- ❖ eye shadow
- ❖ black kajal
- ❖ Blue Eyeliner
- ❖ Lashes Mascara
- ❖ Thick paper
- ❖ Pen
- ❖ Scissors

Method

First start applying an eye cream to relieve any dryness in the under eye area. Gently use the ring finger to apply and blend the product. Allow it to be absorbed, and then apply concealer. If you have very pigmented eyelids, then it is best to use a corrector prior to the application of the concealer. Set the concealer with powder to avoid creases and fine lines. Then pick a green eye shadow and apply it to the whole eyelid area of your eyes. It is best to use a flat brush and pat the color to build good intensity. you can tweak the finish to shimmery or satin.

Next draw a curved one and a half inch scalloped-like pattern on a piece of paper and cut it carefully with a scissor. Use a sharp scissor for creating neat and clean corners in the eye makeup. It will act as a stencil for the eye makeup. The curves need not be very perfect as it is an eye makeup and imperfections too will add a special touch to your overall look. try to keep it similar in size for a neat and even finish. Cut out the design in a rectangular shape as it will help to keep it in place while working with it on the eyes.

Next , gently place the stencil over your eye lid area near the upper lash line. check your stencil fits the entire eyelid area starting from the inner corner of the eyes to the outermost corner. Apply liquid liner and slowly fill in the gaps in the cut out design. After applying the liner, just wait for 3 seconds to allow the liner to dry out completely .you do not have to hold the stencil on your eyes for a long time. Then, slowly remove the stencil and there you have gorgeous scalloped eye makeup. you can easily make desired shapes . then curl your eye lashes with curler and apply mascara to create thicker eyelashes.

It is really very simple eye makeup ,try it.

Dramatic Cut Crease Arabic Eye Makeup

Let's start the eye makeup. Start with clean and fresh eyes. Apply a good eye cream to hydrate the delicate eye area. Conceal all your dark circles with a heavy duty concealer. Use the concealer to hide and lighten my dark circles. Use a thin pointed eye liner brush for creating an intense cut crease look. Brush is very fine and pointed for drawing neat and precise lines.

 Start by drawing a line by following the natural crease of your eyes. Then draw the line completely till the top outer corner of the eyes, and start dropping it slightly. To offer an angle like look, draw a winged eye line. This will lend a nice dramatic definition to your eye shape.

Then, bring the line downward gently by creating shorter and smaller strokes, and connect the line to the outermost corner of your upper lash line. You could use a pencil brush to achieve this step perfectly. Then, fill in the outermost corner of the eye with the same kajal to create a smoky effect for the eye makeup. You can choose a blue, green or purple eye shadow. Apply a light golden colored shimmery eye shadow to the center of the eyelid.

Apply a matte black eye shadow over the areas where the kajal was applied to set it and to avoid creasing. Then, use a small pointed blending brush, and blend the gold and matte black eye shadows Blend it softly with the gold and black eye shadow, using a blending brush.

Apply the same dark teal color eye shadow to the lower lash line. Then, apply mascara and line your eyes to complete the look. This eye makeup is very bold and dramatic. If you want to go for a lighter look, shift the color from black to brown.

....